Bell's Cathedrals

The Cathedral Church of Manchester

A Short History and Description of the Church and of the Collegiate Buildings now known as Chetham's Hospital

Rev. Thomas Perkins

Alpha Editions

This edition published in 2021

ISBN : 9789354756511

Design and Setting By
Alpha Editions
www.alphaedis.com
Email - info@alphaedis.com

As per information held with us this book is in Public Domain.
This book is a reproduction of an important historical work. Alpha Editions uses the best technology to reproduce historical work in the same manner it was first published to preserve its original nature. Any marks or number seen are left intentionally to preserve its true form.

Contents

PREFACE.	- 1 -
CHAPTER I.	- 2 -
CHAPTER II.	- 9 -
CHAPTER III	- 17 -
CHAPTER IV.	- 45 -
DIMENSIONS OF MANCHESTER CATHEDRAL.	- 49 -
CHETHAM'S HOSPITAL AND LIBRARY.	- 52 -
GROUND-PLAN OF THE COLLEGIATE BUILDINGS, NOW CHETHAM'S HOSPITAL.	- 71 -
FOOTNOTES	- 73 -

PREFACE.

I have to acknowledge with my sincerest thanks the help I received locally in compiling this little volume.

The Dean of Manchester was good enough to offer to read the proof-sheets, and has made various suggestions and additions which have done much to improve it. The sheets have also had the benefit of Canon Hicks' revision.

The photographic illustrations, with the exception of two by Mr. W. H. Bowman of Manchester, were taken by myself, and I have also to thank the Dean for permission to photograph in all parts of the church.

Mr. Walter T. Browne, Governor of Chetham's Hospital and Library, gave me every facility for examining and photographing the building, and supplied me with much valuable information. He also carefully revised the proof-sheets of the latter portion of the book.

Mr. J. T. Chapman, of Albert Square, placed his dark-room at my disposal, so that I was able to develop my negatives on the spot, and make second exposures when necessary.

Lastly, Mr. Thackeray Turner, Secretary of the Society for the Protection of Ancient Buildings, lent me sundry papers and reports dealing with Chetham's Hospital and Library. The kind assistance thus received has made my task an easy one, and has materially added to the accuracy of the volume.

THOMAS PERKINS.

TURNWORTH, *September 1901*.

CHAPTER I.

HISTORY OF THE BUILDING.

In the minds of most Englishmen the name of Manchester calls up the image of a vast city that, with the borough of Salford, which, though municipally distinct, yet is topographically united with it, contains a population of about three quarters of a million of inhabitants. And it is, moreover, generally supposed that Manchester is entirely of modern growth—a collection of mills, and warehouses, and shops; yet, if anyone pauses for a moment to consider, the name itself suggests that the foundation of the city must date back from the time of the Roman occupation of the island. It has been, and not unreasonably, supposed that it was a British stronghold before the soldiers of Agricola took possession of it. Certain it is that it was occupied by Roman troops, and it is said that they made their summer camp near the spot where the building that is the subject of this book now stands, hard by the junction of the little stream of the Irk with the larger river Irwell. In those early days these streams in all probability ran bright and clear through broad meadow lands, and were crossed by bridges of very ancient construction. The remains of one such bridge have long been known to exist, and have on more than one occasion been uncovered.

The Irk now runs through a tunnel, and discharges its waters into the grimy, sluggish stream of the Irwell, which divides Manchester from Salford, and runs between the Exchange Station of the London and North-Western Railway and the cathedral church of the new diocese created in 1847.

Many Roman coins, principally those of Nero, Vitellius, Vespasian, Domitian, Trajan, Hadrian, Antoninus Pius, and Constantine, have been found at various times in the course of digging the foundations of houses.

What befell Manchester when the Romans left Britain we do not know. That Paulinus preached here is highly probable; that Ine, King of the West Saxons, resided here with his Queen Ethelburga about 690 is recorded; that, like many other places not far distant from the seaboard, it was ravaged by the Danes is certain. King Edward the Unconquered, in 923, sent troops to repair its walls and garrison the town.

No picturesque legends about the foundation of the original Church of St. Mary which stood near the site of the present cathedral have come down to us. All we know is, that two wood-built churches are mentioned in Domesday Book as standing either in the town or the parish, one of them dedicated to St. Mary, the other to St. Michael.[1] The former was probably a predecessor of the present building, which is dedicated jointly to St. Mary, St. George, and St. Denys, though not on the same site. But of any Norman church of St. Mary not a trace is left, nor are there any remains of thirteenth century work visible in the church as we see it to-day. Various examples of thirteenth and fourteenth century work, however, have been found in the walls of the church and in the western tower at different times during repairs and restorations.

William the Conqueror conferred the lands between the Mersey and the Ribble on Roger of Poictou, who granted the Manor of Manchester to the Gresley family; Thomas Gresley, Baron of Manchester, granted a charter to the townspeople of Manchester in 1301. Under these early barons the church was held successively by about fifteen rectors, among whom may be mentioned William de la Marcia (1284), who became Bishop of Bath and Wells in 1292; Walter Langton, who was appointed Rector of Manchester, and also Keeper of the Great Seal by Edward I. in 1292, and was consecrated Bishop of Lichfield in 1296, but retained his rectory for three years after his consecration; John de Verdun or Everden (1313), who became Dean of St. Paul's in 1323. Meanwhile, the manor had passed from the Gresleys to the De la Warres; the last of their family became a priest, and appointed himself Rector of Manchester in 1373. He was a liberal benefactor to the church, and in order that there should be a suitable body of clergy to look after the spiritual welfare of the town, he endowed the church as a collegiate institution, obtaining the requisite charter from Henry V. in 1422. The college consisted of a warden, eight fellows in priests' orders, four deacons, and six boy choristers.

The old baronial hall was granted to the newly appointed body as a place of residence. This was largely modified to suit the requirements of its new inmates, and the church itself was gradually reconstructed. Hence we find the church built in the Perpendicular style, a style that has been imitated in the many additions that have been made to the building since it was raised to cathedral rank in 1847. So quickly does the smoke-laden atmosphere of Manchester discolour the stone, that in a very few years after their erection the new parts of the church match in colour the older parts of the building, and the passer-by who gives but a casual glance at the cathedral would be surprised to learn how much of its structure dates from the nineteenth century. At the present time, 1901, the only obviously new part is the western porch, but the north and south porches, the Fraser Chapel on the south side of the choir, the south-west corner of the building, as well as the tower, are all modern additions or reconstructions, and much of the exterior has been recased with stone. The residence of the warden and fellows, much modified at subsequent dates, may still be found on the north side of the church, on the other side of a road that skirts the churchyard. It is now known as Chetham's Hospital and Library; for fuller information about this building the reader is referred to the latter part of this volume.

No sooner had the first warden, John Huntington, been appointed, than he set to work to enlarge and beautify the collegiate church.

The oldest part of the church is the arch leading into the Lady Chapel, which, with its responds, has more resemblance to the Decorated than to the Perpendicular style. This arch was accurately restored some twenty-five or thirty years ago. The rebus of Sir John Huntington, the first warden, who was appointed in 1422, renders it probable that this part of the church was largely reconstructed by him. While he was warden, 1422-1458, the choir and its aisles were rebuilt, and the chapter house built. Under successive wardens the work of reconstruction was carried on, and occupied about a hundred years. The third warden, Ralph Langley (1465-1481), is said to have completed the nave; much work was done during the wardenship of James Stanley II. (1485-1509), afterwards Bishop of Ely, for the chapel of the Holy Trinity was founded by W. Radcliffe in 1498; the Jesus Chapel, now the vestry and library, was founded by Richard Beswick in 1506; the Hulme Chapel, now destroyed, which formerly projected to the south from the eastern part of the south wall of the Jesus Chapel, was founded by Ralph Hulme in 1507; the St. James' Chantry or Ducie Chapel was built in the same year; and the choir stalls were erected by the warden himself in 1508. In this year also W. Galley built St. George's Chapel. James Stanley is also recorded to have built the double entrance into the chapter house. The Derby and Ely Chapels on the north side are of rather later date; in the latter the ex-warden, James Stanley II., then Bishop of Ely, was buried. This chapel was built by Sir John Stanley in 1515. In 1518 the eighth warden, George West (1518-1535) is recorded to have built the Lady Chapel, but this work was probably a reconstruction rather than a fresh building; the windows that we see in it now are eighteenth century work, but probably are imitations of those that previously existed in this chapel, and their style indicates a considerably earlier date than 1518. Indeed, their tracery resembles fourteenth century work. It will be noticed from the dates just given that the church was finished not long before the Reformation.

Up to 1541 Manchester belonged to the diocese of Lichfield, but Henry VIII. then transferred it to the newly founded see of Chester.

The college was dissolved by Edward VI., who bestowed its lands on the Stanley family. Queen Mary re-established the college and gave back its lands, with the exception of the domestic buildings, which still remained in the hands of the Earls of Derby. During the time of the Civil Wars the church suffered in common with many other ecclesiastical buildings.

Richard Heyrick, who had been warden since 1636, was deprived of his office in 1646, but was reinstated in 1660. Some negotiations had been entered into for the sale of the domestic buildings to the trustees under the will of Humphrey Chetham, but the sale was not completed until after the Restoration, when they became the property of the feoffees of the Chetham Hospital and Library.

Subsequently the church shared the same fate as befell most ecclesiastical buildings during the eighteenth century, viz., neglect and injudicious repairs. But it was left to the early part of the nineteenth century to work the greatest havoc on the building. A thorough process of repair, or "beautifying" as it was then called, was set on foot in the year 1815. Galleries were erected in the nave, the various chapels outside the nave aisles were thrown into the main building by the removal of the screens which separated them from the north and south aisles, so that from that time the western half of the church has had double aisles on either side of the nave proper. But worse than this, the whole interior was covered with Roman cement, and that this might adhere more firmly to the stone-work, the walls themselves and the pillars of the main arcade of the nave and the clerestory walls were hacked about in the most shameful way. In this condition the church remained for many years. When the new see of Manchester was erected in 1847, this church was chosen as the cathedral church of the diocese, and before long proposals were made to rebuild or enlarge it, as it was felt by many that it lacked the dignity and size of the old cathedral churches, and, indeed, suffered in comparison with many of the old abbey churches that existed in England, some of which have since that time been raised to cathedral rank. Queen Victoria visited Manchester for the first time in 1851, and to commemorate her visit, Canon Parkinson suggested the rebuilding of the church, and himself headed the subscription list with a donation of £1000, but the proposal did not meet with much favour.

VIEW ACROSS CHOIR FROM THE ELY CHAPEL ABOUT 1850.
From Winkles' "Cathedrals."

At this time the municipal seats at the west end were enclosed by a glass screen; above them was the Chetham gallery, as it was called, its back occupied by the organ and choristers, its front by the schoolboys of Chetham's Hospital. The organ had previously stood on the screen beneath the choir arch, but had been removed to the west for a musical festival held in 1828. This old organ loft was then converted into a pewed gallery, intended for the use of the Chetham feoffees, but was usually occupied by the officers of regiments quartered in Manchester.

In 1858 some repairs, external and internal, were carried out, and shortly after this J. E. Gregan, architect, and David Bell, builder, recommended the rebuilding of the tower. Their advice was taken, the old tower was demolished, and a new tower was designed by J. P. Holden. On 4th August 1864 the foundation stone of the new tower was laid by the Bishop, Dr. Prince Lee. In this ceremony, among others, the present Dean of Manchester, Dr. Maclure, took part, acting as chaplain to the High Sheriff, Sir J. P. Kay Shuttleworth, Bart. The tower was nearly four years in building, and was dedicated on Whitsunday 1868.

In 1872 the Dean, Dr. Cowie, and the canons proposed that a new cathedral church should be built on a new site, but this plan met with little favour. Ten years passed away and then Mr. George Milner and Mr. (afterwards Sir) John William Maclure, churchwardens, and Mr. Thomas Lings, comptroller, advocated a thorough restoration of the existing church; plans were prepared by Mr. Crowther, architect; a meeting was called to consider the matter, and it was resolved to accept and carry out these plans. The roof of the nave was repaired, the old bosses being preserved, the galleries were removed, and it was decided to clear off the Roman cement from the pillars and walls, but it was found that the stone-work beneath had been so much mutilated, that it was resolved to rebuild the main arcade of the nave and the clerestory.

Various donors undertook to defray the cost of rebuilding the different bays. A muniment room containing the celebrated parish registers mentioned by Macaulay, was built in memory of Alderman Graves by his son, and the baptistery, in memory of Thomas Chesters, by his son.

The Derby Chapel was re-roofed. The Earl of Derby, notwithstanding the agreement made in 1774 by which the chapel was handed over to the church on condition that the Earls of Derby should no longer be required to keep it in repair, generously contributed £1000 towards this work. The choir roof was renewed in English oak, but the bosses and carved angels were boiled in oil and replaced. Fortunately the Roman cement could be removed from the walls of the choir more easily than from the nave, and the old stone-work was allowed to stand.

The south porch was erected by James Jardine in 1891; the north porch was built as a memorial to James Craven by his children in 1888. The west or Victoria porch was built in 1900 by subscription raised by the present Dean.

The conical roof of the octagonal chapter house is modern; the chapel to the east of it was built by his widow as a memorial to Dr. James Fraser, the second Bishop of Manchester, who died in 1885.

At the present time, 1901, further building operations are being carried on in the yard on the south side of the church, a new and larger chapter house and vestries being in course of erection.

WINDOWS ON THE SOUTH SIDE.

CHAPTER II.

THE EXTERIOR.

The exterior of the Cathedral Church of Manchester is by no means imposing. The traveller who reaches the city by the London and North-Western Railway and alights at the Exchange Station, will see fronting him what appears to be a large parish church with a western tower. Its walls are grimy with the smoke of the city, and although the building occupies a good site, open on every side save the east, with a large churchyard stretching out on the north and south sides of it, yet few of those who see it would stay their steps to walk round the building or enter it by the south porch, unless they had been previously told that this parish church, as it seemed to them, and as in a certain way it is, is also the Cathedral Church of Manchester, and that its interior is both impressive as a whole, and contains detail work of the highest interest.

Our examination of the exterior may well begin with the most recent addition to the church—**the western porch**—only lately finished and still showing the colour of the stone fresh from the carver's hands. Whether this addition is an improvement to the general appearance of the building or not is open to question. To some, among them the writer, it appears that the porch takes away from the appearance of height in the tower, much as the Galilee Chapel at Durham, beautiful as it is in its details, is an excrescence detracting from the effect of the western front of St. Cuthbert's Cathedral Church. Moreover, the single crocketed turret that rises from the south-west corner of the porch proper gives it a one-sided appearance, which is somewhat to be regretted, as with this exception the porch and its lower flanking chambers is symmetrical, as indeed is the church itself in its main features, turret answering to turret, and window to window, porch to porch. The carving on the western porch is elaborate and carefully executed, and if, as must necessarily be the case owing to the conditions under which nineteenth century carving was executed, it lacks the freedom that is so great a charm in old work, it is more in accordance with the general style of the church, and is characteristic of its own date. This porch was designed by Mr. Basil Champneys, who has succeeded in training carvers to carry out his designs in an admirable manner. A verbal description of the porch is hardly needed, as the illustration on the opposite page will show the reader its character. On either side of the porch is a chamber rising to about the same height as the spring of the arch of the doorway; each of these is flat-roofed, its wall terminates in a pierced battlemented parapet, and is lighted by two rectangular-headed windows facing west. To the south and north of these two chambers respectively, are iron gates and flights of steps giving access to the churchyard.

THE WEST PORCH.

Ascending the southern flight we find before us the west ends of the two south aisles of the church; the roof of the inner one slopes slightly down from the clerestory wall, and the outer one rises into a very obtuse-angled gable. The west end of the inner or true aisle is original, but the outer aisle was extended two bays westward at the time of the recent restoration. The windows of the church, though all or nearly all of Perpendicular character, are not all alike, as may be seen by examining the illustrations; but in most of them the hood moulding after following the curve of the arch at the head of the window, is brought down in a vertical line for a short distance beside the lower part of the window. Most of the windows have four lights, but there are some exceptions, which will be duly noticed as we pass by them. To begin with, the west window of the outer south aisle has five lights. On turning round the south-west corner of this aisle we find the **south porch** projecting from the second bay. The porch itself consists of two bays, and has two stories. The lower story of the porch proper is lighted by two two-light windows on the western side, the upper story by two windows on the western and southern faces, and by one on the eastern face. Beneath the windows on the south side the following inscription may be read:—

> To the honour and Glory of God and in thankful acknowledgement of many mercies this porch is erected by James Jardine of Manchester and Alderley Edge in the year of our Lord MDCCCXCI.

THE SOUTH PORCH.

An octagonal stair turret surmounted by a crocketed pyramidal termination stands at the south angle of the inner bay on the eastern side. The whole of this porch is elaborately carved, as will be seen from the illustration. The next two bays of the south aisle project beyond the general line of the south wall of the church. The walls of this are finished by a pierced battlemented parapet similar to that which runs round the south porch. The windows in these two bays are alike, but the next two in the south wall have five lights, and differ from the last two in their shape and tracery (see illustration, p. 12). To the south of the church about this point stands a sundial, shown in the illustration. The three next bays belong to what was formerly known as the Jesus Chapel. In the westernmost of these there is a doorway to give room for which the sill of the window is placed at a higher level than the sills of the other windows. The tracery of these windows differs from the preceding two. From the easternmost of the three bays of the Jesus Chapel formerly projected the Hulme chantry. To the east of the Jesus Chapel stands the octagonal chapter house; three of its sides contain windows of a pattern differing from any of these already mentioned. From within the parapet, which is not battlemented, rises a rather steep pyramidal roof. This is modern. Whether the original roof was of this form or not is not known, but the modern roof is a distinctly agreeable feature. To the east of the chapter house is another window in the south wall, and then we come to the Fraser Memorial Chapel, which forms the south-east angle of the church. This has a four-light window in its south and a three-light window in its eastern wall. Before examining the east end of the church we may remark that the clerestory wall is terminated by a pierced battlemented parapet—a modern addition—and that the pattern is slightly different on either side of the octagonal turret which rises from the junction of the nave and choir. The parapet that runs along the south wall of the chapel of St. Nicholas, again, differs from that which runs along the other walls on the south side of the church.

The east window of the south choir aisle has five lights; passing this we come to the **Lady Chapel**. This is exceedingly small, projecting only some eighteen feet to the east of the aisle walls. It has two bays, each lit by a small two-light window on either side. Against the centre of the eastern face rises a buttress, on either side of which is a four-light window. As already mentioned in Chapter I. the Lady Chapel windows are eighteenth century work, probably copies of the original windows, and have tracery of Decorated character.

THE ELY CHAPEL.

Beyond the Lady Chapel is the window of the north choir aisle; and beyond this again the eastern termination of the Derby Chapel. This contains a seven-light window. Passing round the north-eastern corner we see the **Ely Chapel** projecting from the second bay to the west, with four-light windows in its eastern and western walls, and a five-light window on its northern face. From the fourth and fifth bays, counting from the east, projects a low building with a battlemented parapet, a door and square headed windows, erected to contain the hydraulic apparatus used for working the bellows of the organ. To the west of this is a small doorway with an ogee head leading into the ante chapel of the Derby or John the Baptist's Chapel. This is the last bay of the eastern division of the church. The next bay, the north wall of what was once St. James' Chapel, contains a five-light window. After two more bays, comprising the chapel of the Holy Trinity, we come to the registry, and see the north porch projecting from the last bay but one. This bears a general resemblance to the south porch, save that niches take the place of windows on the east and west faces of the upper story, and that the stair turret stands on the west side at the angle between the porch and aisle wall.

The following inscription may be read running round the porch commencing on the eastern side.

> "To the glory of God and in loving memory of James Craven this porch and registry are erected by his children 1888."

The west window of the outer north aisle has seven lights, and that of the inner aisle five.

As on the south side so on the north, the tracery is not the same in all the windows. Those on the north side of the Derby Chapel and the Ely Chantry resemble each other; the next is a short window above the doorway; the next, which is known as the Gordon window, is entirely different; the next three have tracery similar to that of the windows of the Derby Chapel.

The parapet along the north walls of the church, like that along the south walls, is pierced and battlemented, the design differing in different parts. The parapet of the Lady Chapel, however, is not pierced, but is simply battlemented. The parapet on the clerestory on both sides is a modern addition, and is considered by some to be no improvement on the old form which ran in an unbroken line from end to end of the church, and gave an appearance of greater length than that given by the present arrangement, with its line broken by battlements and pinnacles. The two octagonal turrets that rise from the east end of the clerestory walls with their crocketed pyramidal terminations form a pleasing feature.

The tower, square in section, projects from the western extremity of the nave, and rises to the stately height of 140 feet. The west window of the nave is surmounted on the outside by a richly carved ogee label; in the next stage we see the faces of the clock, and in the belfry stage above double windows on each face of the tower; a pierced battlemented parapet with three pinnacles at each of the angles and one at the middle points of each of its sides, forms a suitable termination to the tower.

We have now carefully examined the exterior of the church in detail. It remains only to mention the points of view from which it is best seen as a whole. The view from the roadway running up to the railway station shows the tower to advantage, as not only is it of considerable height itself, but its base on the level of the churchyard is considerably raised above the street. The whole of the south side, which is richer in variety and detail than the north, can be well seen from the churchyard, and the north side itself from the open space in front of Chetham's hospital, the play-ground of the boys who are educated there.

NORTH SIDE OF THE NAVE.

THE CHOIR, LOOKING EAST.

THE CHOIR SCREEN.

CHAPTER III

THE INTERIOR.

It has been already said that the exterior of the Cathedral Church at Manchester lacks somewhat of the charm that so many of our old cathedrals possess. There is no wide-spreading close with its smooth turf and immemorial elms, no birds to fly round tower and pinnacle, and break the silence of the home of ancient peace with their songs or cries, but ever we hear the scream of railway engines, the bells of tramcars, and the roar of the traffic along a busy thoroughfare. The surrounding buildings are not now, as in many cathedral cities, the residences of Dean and Canons, quaint and mediaeval, with stone mullioned windows and ivy-covered walls, but modern erections, shops, and warehouses, and hotels. And the church itself, destitute of transept and central tower, provided only with a western tower, gives us the idea of a large parish church, rather than of a building associated in our mind with Bishop, Dean, and Canons. There is no cloister-garth with its surrounding walks, the old collegiate buildings are detached from the church and appropriated to secular purposes; so that probably our first feeling is one of disappointment, but this feeling will vanish as soon as we have passed into its interior. The usual way of entrance is by the south porch; this is always open. The western doors are unfortunately generally closed—unfortunately, for the most impressive view of the church is to be had from beneath the tower arch looking to the east. It is a dimly lighted building; this is due chiefly to two causes: first to the fact that it is enormously wide, and the aisle windows are therefore far from the central nave, and secondly to the fact that almost all the windows both of aisles and clerestory are filled with painted glass, in many cases of a deep colour, and rendered still more impervious to light by the incrustation of carbon deposited on their outside by the perpetual smoke of the city. So dark is the church that in the winter months it has generally to be lit with gas all the day long, and even in the summer, in comparatively bright weather, some gas burners will generally be found alight. The mist also of the exterior atmosphere finds its way into the building, and hangs beneath the roof, lending an air of mystery to the whole place, and giving rise to most beautiful effects when the sunlight streams through the clerestory windows. The tone also of the nave arcading and clerestory rebuilt in recent years, of warm, rose-coloured sandstone, is very lovely.

The visitor on entering the church, before examining the different objects in detail, should get general impressions of the building. The view from just inside the south porch showing the four rows of arcading separating the outer aisles from the inner, and these from the central nave, is very fine. The view from beneath the tower arch looking eastward is most impressive.

Another good view is from the altar steps looking westward, especially in the early part of a bright day, when there is sufficient light to show the magnificent tabernacle work of the stalls, and the organ-stands out clearly defined against the sunlit misty air of the upper part of the nave behind it.

VIEW ACROSS THE NAVE, LOOKING NORTH-EAST.

To see these three views of the building under favourable conditions of light will well repay the visitor for a journey of many miles to Manchester, to say nothing of the exquisite detail work that now demands our attention.

It has been already explained that the outer aisles on either side have been formed by throwing down the walls or screens that once divided these spaces into a series of chapels on the outside of the real nave aisles. In Continental churches double aisles on the north and south side of the church are by no means uncommon, but instances of this arrangement are more rarely met with in England. The most familiar example is Chichester Cathedral, where double aisles have been formed by the inclusion of lateral chapels.

It has been already stated that the baptistery which occupies the western end of the outer southern aisles is entirely modern, as also is the south porch. At one time a small porch called Bibby's Porch projected from the second bay from the west of the true south aisle, to the east of which, stretching right over the outer south aisle, was the Chapel of St. George. This occupied two bays, and projecting from it to the south was Brown's Chantry. To the east of St. George's Chapel, also occupying two bays, was the Chapel of St. Nicholas, the Trafford Chapel. These were the chapels on the south side of the nave aisle. Opposite to them, outside the north nave aisle, were two chapels, that of the Most Holy Trinity at the west, that of St. James, otherwise known as the Ducie Chapel, at the east end. The west wall of the outer nave aisle on the north side is original, so that the whole length of the series of chapels on this side was greater than that of the series on the south side. The nave and its twin aisles, as will be seen from what has already been said, consist of six bays. The eastern half of the church also consists of six bays, and the choir aisles, like those of the nave, are flanked by chapels which have fortunately remained undestroyed down to the present day, enclosed by their original screens. On the south side, raised three steps above the level of the nave and occupying three bays, was the Jesus Chapel, now divided into two parts, the western bay being used as a vestry, the two others as the Cathedral Library; from this a door leads into the chapter house, the main entrance to which is from the choir aisle. With this the unbroken series of building attached to the south side of the church ends, but from the easternmost bay a doorway in a screen opens into the Fraser Chapel, built as a memorial to her husband, the second Bishop of Manchester, by Mrs. Fraser. Crossing the church by the ambulatory, passing the small Lady Chapel, we find the whole length of the outer aisle on the north side occupied by the chapel of St. John the Baptist, often called the Derby Chapel. The western bay forms the antechapel, from which we pass into the chapel itself through the original oak screen. From the second bay, counting from the east end of this, the Ely Chapel projects.

THE INNER SOUTH AISLE OF THE NAVE.

The reader should follow on the plan the general description just given, and while doing so he will notice that the church is not quite regularly built, but tapers slightly towards the east. The enclosed choir, presbytery, and sanctuary taper still more, so that the east end is between three and four feet narrower than the west end. But this enclosed space is symmetrically placed in the church. The plan shows the very great width of the church in proportion to its length. The interior width of the nave and its double aisles is 114 feet, while its length is only 85 feet; the whole interior length of the church, omitting the tower at the west and the Lady Chapel at the east, is 172 feet. This shows that the choir is about the same length as the nave, and that the total length of nave and choir is only about one and a half times the width.

THE TOWER ARCH.

Having now taken a cursory glance round the church, we will go once more over the same ground, examining it more in detail. We will suppose that the outer doors of the **West Porch** are open, and we can pass through them from the street. We go up from the level of the pavement three steps and find ourselves within the porch; on the south and north sides of it, doors open into two rooms used the one as the lecture-room of the Scholae Episcopi (or non-residential Theological College of the Diocese), the other as a schoolroom for the choir boys. A flight of eleven steps takes us up to a landing measuring about five feet from west to east, and then four more steps bring us to the level of the nave floor, and we enter through what were originally the west doors of the church, into the space below the tower. The ceiling of this is of fan tracery, and its side walls are panelled in five tiers. Passing under the tower arch and looking back, we notice that the tower arch with the walls on either side of it are original. **The Baptistery** is a modern addition. The font formerly stood in the outer aisle on the north side. The **South Porch** is also new. It is divided into two bays, each covered with a vault formed of eight ribs crossing each other at the centre, and decorated by two lierne ribs in each of the four quarters. The arcade dividing the outer from the inner aisle on the south side is entirely modern; the chapels which occupied the site of the outer aisle were formerly divided from each other by stone walls, and from the aisle by irregular arches filled with oak screens. All these were removed in 1815, so as to throw the area of the chapels into that of the church; an arcade was then built, but this was removed to make room for the present arcade during the restoration that was begun in 1872. The westernmost chantry, or **Chapel of St. George**, was founded by W. Galley in 1508. The next, the chapel of **St. Nicholas**, or the Trafford Chantry, is said to have been founded long ere the present church was built in 1186 by Robert de Greslet; at the south-east corner of this a piscina may be seen, though the altar has disappeared. Three steps and a screen divide this chantry from the larger **Jesus Chapel**. This is separated from the south aisle by a beautiful wooden screen of sixteenth century date. This is glazed in order to make the room now used as a library comfortable. This chantry was founded in 1506.

SCREEN BETWEEN THE JESUS CHAPEL AND THE SOUTH CHOIR AISLE.

ENTRANCE TO THE CHAPTER HOUSE, SOUTH CHOIR AISLE.

THE SOUTH CHOIR AISLE.

Between the Jesus Chapel and the entrance to the chapter house on the south wall of the aisle are memorial tablets to Richard Heyrick, warden, who died in 1667, and Thomas Ogden, who died in 1763. The entrance to the **Chapter House** is a very beautiful piece of work. There are two doorways whose heads are four centred arches; above these there are two tiers of panel work, all being enclosed by one large arch whose sides and top are decorated by six tiers of panelling on each side (see illustration, p. 32). The chapter house is very comfortably fitted up. There are to be seen in it several fragments of brasses and of other old work taken from the floor of the choir and of the Lady Chapel and elsewhere.

The **Fraser Chapel** contains an altar cenotaph in memory of the second Bishop of Manchester, who died October 22nd, 1885, at Bishop's Court, Higher Broughton, Manchester, but who was buried, not in his cathedral church, but in the churchyard of Ufton Nervet in Berkshire, a parish of which he had once been rector. The recumbent statue is considered to be a fine likeness of the late bishop. This statue was unveiled on July 8th, 1887.

The tomb bears the following inscription written by the late Dr Vaughan, Dean of Llandaff.

> "To the beloved memory of James Fraser, D.D., Bishop of Manchester, 1870-85, a man of singular gifts both of nature and the spirit; brave, true, devout, diligent, in labours unwearied. He won all hearts by opening to them his own, and so administered this great Diocese as to prove yet once more that the people know the voice of a good shepherd and will follow where he leads."

At the east end of the south aisle stands a marble life-size statue by Bailey of Thomas Fleming, who died in 1848, and a memorial tablet to the Rev. George Ogden, B.D., who died in 1706. The aisle is divided from the choir by a wooden screen; in the third bay from the east are iron gates leading into the choir. The retro-choir, about thirteen feet from east to west, runs between the back of the modern reredos behind the high altar and the beautiful mediaeval screen which stands beneath the arch at the entrance to the Lady Chapel. The **Lady Chapel** has modern fittings making it suitable for the celebration of Holy Communion when the congregation is small. In the south wall a piscina may be noticed, and on the north side of the altar stands a Renaissance font of grey-veined marble which was formerly in use in the nave. There are marble tablets in memory of various members of the Chetham family at the west ends of the north and south walls of the Lady Chapel.

SCREEN OF THE LADY CHAPEL.

On the west wall of the arch leading into the chapel may be seen the rebus of Sir John Huntington, the first warden and rebuilder of the church. On the north side is a man and dog *hunting*, on the south side two *tuns* of wine. This rebus is repeated in the roof of the choir. At the north-east corner of the north choir aisle may be seen a statue by Theed (1853) of Humphrey Chetham, the founder of the Hospital (*i.e.* school) and Library that bears his name. He sits, a roll in his right hand, with long hair and pointed beard, a ruff round his neck, and a long cloak which, falling open in front, shows doublet and slashed trunk hose. At the bottom of the pedestal sits one of the boys of the hospital school, pointing with his left hand to a book which he holds open in his right, on which we read the inscription: "He hath dispersed abroad, and given to the poor, and his righteousness remaineth for ever" (Ps. cxii. 9; Prayer-book version).

STATUE OF SIR HUMPHREY CHETHAM.

An old oak screen running under five arches of the arcading to the north side of the aisle separates the **Derby Chapel** from the aisle. This screen is of good design, but the workmanship is not so good as that of the other old screens in the church. Near the first pier, counting from the east, is the altar tomb of Hugh Birley, M.P. for Manchester, with a recumbent figure. Here also may be seen an old oak deed chest. About halfway down this aisle on the south side may be seen a small organ built by the celebrated Father Smith, dated 1680; this is of the finest tone and is still frequently used. It has one manual with seven stops and pedal with one stop.

Four steps lead from the outer nave aisle on the north side into the antechapel that stands to the west end, outside the entrance to the Derby Chapel.

This chapel is dedicated to St. John the Baptist. It was a private chantry built and endowed by the Stanley family, of which the Earls of Derby were members. Two of the family were closely connected with the church. One, James Stanley, Prebendary of St. Paul's, and archdeacon of Chester, held the office of warden from 1481-1485, and was succeeded by another James Stanley, whose tenure was longer, 1485-1509. He it was who began the building of the Derby Chapel. He became bishop of Ely, but when he died in 1515 his body was buried at Manchester, close by the screen of the **Ely Chapel**; but "for reasons which need not be mentioned here" his body was laid just by the wall, and the chapel was erected by his son according to his will over his grave, and called after the name of his diocese. This tomb still stands there, with its original brass and curiously inscribed epitaph, for which see hereafter.

The following description is copied from a MS in Chetham's Library.

> "In the old or Christ's Church, Manchester, is a Chapell dedicated to S. John Baptist on the screen which separates it from the broad north aisle and over door leading from the aforesaid chapel into the aisle is an ancient coat of arms carv'd in wood, and three old brass inscriptions setting forth the founders of the chapell together with ye cause of its erection.
>
> "The arms are those of Stanley tho much different from those born by that name at this day tho unquestionably of the same family with the present Earl of Derby, who bears 3 stags heads caboch'd on a bend these arms on the screen bears the stags heads in chief and 3 eagles claws in base this kind of bearing might possibly be to difference it from the elder house or grand stem of the family, a matter not unusual in those days. In an old manuscript I have the above arms born by the name of Stanley of Handford, and from this family of Handford I should suppose sprung Sr John Stanley of Aderley Ches^r which is within a few miles of Handford tho S^r J^{no} now bears the same arms for his

paternall coat as the Earl of Derby. The arms impal'd with Stanley on the screen is first and fourth a Chevron between three mascles voided second and third a star with seven points the whole arms appears to be totally void of colouring. The helmet is very clumsy and differs much from those now us'd in arms. The crest or rather part of a crest for it appears to have had something broke from it is not now to be determin'd what it formerly was. What I take to be the motto is grav'd upon two plates of brass on each side the arms the half of one brass is broke way but no doubt was the same as the other they are engraved in the old text with these words Vanitas vanitatum Oiā Vanitas that is Vanity of vanity all is vanity.

"On the brass plate over the door is grav'd in the same character and old Latin Obsecramus ut adjuvetis nos Jacobū Stanley Eliens Epis Johāne Stanley milite et Margareta uxore ej ac parētes cor oracionibus vris apud Domˉ Jhesū expmˉ q. hanc Capellā in ej nomine et in honore Sancti Johanis Baptiste Fabricavimus Anº incarnationis illius MCCCCXIII. Designs from the Originall plates may be seen in the following drawings. The Inscription on the long brass I take to be this in English.

"We beseech you that you assist us James Stanley Bishop of Ely John Stanley Knt. and Margaret his wife and their parents with your prayers to yᵉ Lord Jesus Christ who have built this chapel in his name and in honour of St Jnº Baptist in the year of his incarnation 1513."

According to an old poem entitled Flodden Field Sʳ John Stanley was at that great Battle fought in Sept. 1513 along with other gentlemen of Lancashire and Cheshire and in enumerating the Leaders says:

Next with Sir John Stanley there yede

The Bishop of Ely's servants bold

Sir Lionel Percy eke did lead

Some hundred men well tried and told.

    (Barrett MS. No. 41458, C. 4. 13.)

INTERIOR OF NORTH DOORWAY.

These two chapels were the private property of the Earls of Derby, who had to keep them in repair. In the second half of the eighteenth century the roofs needed extensive repair; this was done by the thirteenth Earl of Derby in conjunction with the townspeople of Manchester, and the Earl surrendered his rights to the chapels, handing them over to the parishioners on condition that he and his successors should no longer be held responsible for keeping them in repair. The Derby Chapel is now fitted with an altar at the east end, a font on the north side, and oak benches, so that it can be used for week-day services when desired. The Ely Chapel is not fitted in any way.

VIEW ACROSS THE NAVE, LOOKING NORTH-WEST.

St. James' Chapel, or the Ducie Chantry, and the **Chapel Of the Holy Trinity**, which formerly occupied the east and west ends of what is now the outer north aisle, and were founded, the former in 1507 and the latter by W. Radcliffe of Ordsall in 1498, have no longer any separate existence; the only sign of their having been chapels that remains is a piscina in the pier at the south east corner of St. James' Chapel. The arcade between the outer and inner north aisles originally dated from about 1500.

The North or Craven Porch is opposite to the south porch and bears a strong resemblance to it. It consists of two bays, each vaulted in stone in the same manner as the bays of the south or Jardine Porch; a door to the east side of the inner bay leads into the registry office.

It now remains to examine the **Central Nave** and **Choir**. This church differs from most of our cathedral and abbey churches in having no triforium.[2] And the clerestory is not lofty, so that the church is rather low for its width,[3] though the height of the arches of the main arcade prevents this being felt. The roofs of the aisles are all modern, but that of the nave, though extensively repaired, has much of the original work in it, and, with the exception of a few bosses, the choir roof is old. All the roofs are of timber; in the nave the intersections of the main beams are covered by beautiful bosses carved out of the solid wood. On either side, at the points from which the main cross beams spring, is a series of angelic figures splendidly carved in wood: those on the south side playing stringed instruments, those on the north side wind instruments.

The choir roof is more ornate; the panels between the beams are filled with tracery; the bosses here are differently constructed from those in the nave; here each leaf was separately carved and then nailed in its place. At the time of the restoration this roof was skilfully repaired by introducing new beams above the old ones and fastening the old to the new with bolts.

The pillars of the main arcade of the nave are modern work built in imitation of the original ones. They are light and graceful, and like many other pillars of fifteenth century date, are formed of shafts of which only half have separate capitals, the other mouldings running round the arch. The spaces between the arches are elaborately carved with heraldic shields.

THE CHOIR, LOOKING WEST.

DESK-ENDS IN THE CHOIR STALLS; NORTH SIDE.

Towards the east end of the nave may be seen desks for the choir on either side, a brass eagle lectern on the south side, and a modern pulpit against the first pillar from the east on the north side (see page 54). The pulpit, the gift of the late Chancellor Christie and his wife, is octagonal, and six of its faces are carved with representations of Christ, the four Evangelists, and St. Paul; of the other two sides one rests against the pier, and the other, on the north, forms the entrance from the pulpit steps. The ancient rood screen (see page 23) is a very beautiful piece of work. It has three wide openings with double doors in each; upon it stands the central part of the large organ; other parts of the organ occupy spaces in the north and south aisles behind the stalls. The case was designed by Sir Gilbert Scott, and is effective.

CHOIR STALLS, NORTH SIDE.

The present **organ** rebuilt by Wadsworth Brothers at the cost of Sir W. H. Houldsworth, Bart., 1871, has

Four manuals CC to A	58	notes
Pedal CCC to F	30	"
The great organ has	13	stops
swell	16	"
choir	8	"
solo	5	"

pedal	9	"
accessory	8	"
and combination pedals	8	"

If we pass on through the screen beneath the organ we find ourselves in the **choir**. This, the choir proper, as distinguished from the presbytery to the east of it, is sometimes called the Radcliffe choir, for many members of this family were buried here, and their brasses were placed on the floor, but these were removed when the floor was repaved with tiles. On either side of us, and behind us, we see some of the most elaborate tabernacle work to be met with anywhere. Some idea may be formed of the wealth of detail by examining the illustration on the opposite page. There are twelve stalls on either side, and three on each side of the entrance through the rood screen facing east. The stalls are furnished with misereres, which, in common with many others both in England and on the Continent, represent all manner of quaint subjects, monsters, animals, hunting scenes, etc.

The **stalls** date from the early part of the sixteenth century, and bear a strong resemblance to those in Beverley Minster and Ripon Cathedral. At Beverley, however, the level cornice above the canopies which we see at Manchester is wanting, except at the west end.

The carved elbows of the stalls and the ends of the book desks are also worthy of careful examination, especially the Eagle and Child and general carving of the Dean's Stall, which is a marvel of beautiful workmanship, and said by high authorities to be unequalled.

Between the stalls the floor is one step higher than that of the nave, and at the east end of the stalls there is a further rise of two steps as we pass into the presbytery. Here, on the south side, we see the bishop's throne—modern work, carved with a view to be in harmony with the stalls, but comparing unfavourably with them in execution. There is a rise of two more steps into the sanctuary, and the altar itself is raised two steps higher; this gives a good effect. Behind the altar is an elaborately carved wooden reredos of modern work, richly painted and gilt. The upper part, as will be seen from the illustration on p. 22, is wider than the lower; it is divided vertically into seven divisions, the two lateral divisions on each side being themselves divided into two tiers. The three central niches contain figures of the three patron saints, St. George on the north, the Blessed Virgin in the centre, and St. Denys on the south side.[4] Above the central figure, St. Mary, is another niche containing a seated figure of Christ, holding in His left hand an orb and cross, His right hand raised in the act of blessing; above this figure is a canopy. On the top of the six uprights that form the vertical divisions of the reredos, angels stand with clasped hands. The carving on the smaller panels illustrates the following verses of the "Preface to the Sanctus" which are inscribed beneath them.

| "With angels and we laud and | archangels and magnify Thy | all the company glorious name. | of heaven Amen." |

It will be noticed that there are no sedilia in the usual place on the south side of the altar, the arch being open where we might expect to find them, and there is no pulpit in the choir. Most of the services in which a sermon is preached are conducted in the nave.

Most of the windows have in recent times been filled with painted glass. Perhaps we may be inclined to think that there are too many thus filled, and that it would have been well if the windows of the clerestory had been left uncoloured. Certain it is that as there is no triforium, there is no place from which the clerestory windows can be examined; and had they been left unpainted, the church would have been much lighter than it is.

A brief description must now be given of the windows. We will begin with the west window in the tower, proceeding eastward along the outer south aisle, crossing the church by the ambulatory, and coming back to the west by the aisle on the north side, and then examining the clerestory windows of nave and choir.

The Windows.—The west window of the tower has five lights, and is divided by one transom. It represents the Ascension, and Acts of Mercy. It was given by J. C. Harter, and is the work of Hardman.

The west window of the inner aisle on the south side has four lights, and its subject is the parable of the Good Samaritan. It was erected by subscription in memory of Jonas Craven, and was painted by Messrs. Heaton, Butler & Baynes.

The west window of the outer south aisle, or Baptistery, has six lights, and represents baptism by blood, water, and fire, illustrated by the martyrdom of St. Stephen, the baptism of Christ, and the descent of the Holy Ghost at Pentecost. It was given by Thomas Chesters in 1892, and is the work of Messrs. Percy Bacon & Bros.

The window in the westernmost bay of the outer south aisle has four lights, and illustrates the text "Suffer little children to come unto Me," and was erected as a memorial to W. H. Bowler (son-in-law of Thomas Chesters), who died in 1887. This also was painted by Percy Bacon & Bros.

The window to the east of the porch in the Brown Chapel has four lights, and represents Christ healing all manner of sickness, and was erected in memory of John, William, Maria, and Henry Stevenson, and is by Wailes of Newcastle.

The next window has four lights, and has for its subject various incidents in the life of St. John the Baptist: 1, the announcement of his birth to Zacharias; 2, his birth; 3, his preaching in the wilderness; and 4, his baptism of Christ. This was given by Margaret Clowes in memory of the Rev. T. Clowes, and is by Hardman.

The window in the fifth bay has five lights. It represents Christ in Glory, and was given by Catharine, Countess of Stamford and Warrington, in memory of her husband, the seventh Earl, who died in 1883. It was painted by Messrs. Clayton & Bell.

The next window also has five lights, and illustrates the Magnificat. It was erected by public subscription in memory of Dean Oakley, who died in 1890. It is by Burlison & Grylls.

The next window is in the westernmost bay of the Jesus Chapel. It has four lights. Its subject is Simeon receiving Christ in the temple. It was given as a memorial to Frederick Andrews, who died in 1890. It is by Messrs. Heaton, Butler & Baynes.

The next window, in that part of the Jesus Chapel now used as the cathedral library, has four lights, and represents Christ among the doctors; it is a memorial to James Gray, who died in 1871, and is by Messrs. Heaton, Butler & Baynes.

The next window of four lights has for its subject Christ healing all manner of disease, and was inserted in memory of Jonas Craven, who died in 1894. It is by Messrs. Heaton, Butler & Baynes.

There are four windows in the chapter house, all of four lights. The first, with figures of Sts. James, Thomas, Simon, and Jude, was given by Canon Gibson in 1869, and is by Messrs. Ward & Hughes. The next, representing Sts. Peter, Mary, George, and Paul, is by Edmundson & Son, and incorporates some old glass found in the clerestory windows of the choir. The next, with figures of Sts. Matthew, Mark, Luke, and John, was given by the children of Canon Wray, in memory of their father, who died in 1866. It is the work of Clayton & Bell. The last, with figures of Sts. James, Andrew, Philip, and Bartholomew, was given by Dean Bowers in 1869, and is by Ward & Hughes.

In the bay between the chapter house and the Fraser Chapel is a four-light window with eight subjects. In the upper row, The Transfiguration, Lazarus,

Christ riding on an Ass, The institution of the Lord's Supper; and in the lower, "This is my beloved Son," Elisha raising the Child, David, The offering of Isaac. This was given in 1859 by a citizen once a chorister. It is by Edmundson & Son.

In the Fraser Chapel are two windows. The first, facing south, has four lights, and contains the glass which formerly occupied the window of the bay that was opened out when the Fraser Chapel was built. Its four subjects are: Simeon, The Baptism of Christ, The Miracle at Cana, and Christ blessing little Children. An inscription records that it was given in 1858 by a citizen once a chorister; it is by Edmundson & Son.

The window in the east wall of this chapel has three lights. Its subjects are: 1, St. John; 2, "I am He that was dead and am alive again"; 3, St. Paul. It was erected as a memorial to Bishop Fraser by Messrs. Shrigley & Hunt.

The east window of the south choir aisle has five lights, and each of these contains two subjects.

In the upper row we see Christ in the centre, with two of the evangelists on either side of him. In the lower tier are represented: 1, The Agony in the Garden; 2, Christ bearing His Cross; 3, The Crucifixion; 4, The Angels announcing the Resurrection; 5, The Ascension. This was given by G. Pilkington, and is by Wailes of Newcastle.

In the Lady Chapel there are two windows, each of two lights in the north and south walls, and two, of four lights each, in the east wall.

Beginning with the westernmost window in the south side, we find a representation of the descent of the Holy Ghost on the day of Pentecost, and an inscription which states that the window is a memorial to "John Allen bonorum bujus ecclesiae custos," who died in 1861.

The next window contains a representation of Christ among the Doctors. It is a memorial to Samuel Bulteel, who died in 1883.

The next window in the east wall represents the Crucifixion of Christ and the two robbers, and was erected to commemorate the fact that the Lady Chapel was once the property of the Hoare family.

The other window in this wall shows the visit of the Magi, and was given by J. H. Chetham in 1884, in memory of Humphrey Chetham, the great benefactor to Manchester, who was born in 1580 and died in 1653.

The two windows in the north wall represent the Annunciation and Salutation respectively, and were inserted as memorials to Edith Mary Romilly, daughter of Dean Cowie, who died in 1883; it was given by the

Dean; and to Elizabeth Sharp, who died in 1881. The latter was given by S. Wm., and Elizabeth Bulteel.

All the windows in the Lady Chapel are by Moore of London.

The five-light window at the east end of the north choir aisle illustrates the text beginning "I was hungry," etc. It was given by G. Pilkington as a memorial to Humphrey Chetham. It is by Wailes of Newcastle.

The east window of the Derby Chapel has seven lights, each containing two subjects. The upper tier are: 1, The Magi; 2, The flight into Egypt; 3 and 5, Angels; 4, Christ; 6, Christ blessing Children; 7, Christ among the Doctors.

In the lower tier the three central subjects are hidden by the reredos erected in recent years over the altar. Of the four visible, the first is the raising of Jairus' daughter; 3, Christ setting a Child in the midst; 6, Suffer little Children to come unto Me; 7, The feeding of the Five Thousand. It is by Edmundson & Son of Manchester.

The easternmost window in the north wall has four lights. The subjects are: St. Mary, "Why weepest thou?" and St. John. This window was inserted as a memorial to George Hull Bowers, D.D., the second Dean of Manchester, who died in 1872. It is by Burlison & Grylls.

There are three windows in the Ely Chantry. That facing north has five lights, the other two four; the central light of the north window contains the figure of Bishop Stanley wearing his mitre and holding his pastoral staff.

The next window to the west contains in its four lights representation of four incidents in the life of Jacob: His dream, Rachel tending her sheep, Jacob watering them, and Jacob's journey into Egypt. This window is a memorial to William Newall, who died in 1851. It is by Ward & Hughes.

The next window, also of four lights, represents Christ cleansing the leper, raising the daughter of Jairus, blessing children, and restoring sight to Bartimaeus. This was inserted in memory of Robert Barnes, who died in 1871. It is by Clayton & Bell.

The next window—the last within the screen of the Derby Chapel—represents: 1. Jacob blessing Ephraim and Manasseh (Gen. xlviii. 14); 2, The end of Job (Job xlii. 17); 3, Simeon blessing Christ (Luke ii. 27-29); 4, The great multitude in Heaven (Rev. vii. 9.) It is a memorial window to Thomas Broadbent, who died in 1875. It was given by his daughter, Elizabeth Boyd Garfit, the wife of Thomas Garfit, M.P. for Bristol, and is by Hardman.

In the antechapel is a four light window. The subjects are the Good Shepherd teaching the young and healing the sick. It was given by James Chadwick, churchwarden, in 1863, and is by Ward & Hughes.

THE GORDON MEMORIAL WINDOW.

The easternmost window in the nave, in what was once the Ducie Chapel, has five lights, and was erected by C. J. Scholfield in 1888 as a memorial to Major-General Gordon, who was killed at Khartoum in 1888. In the centre light the General is represented with his hand on the head of a native boy; in the other lights we see native women and children expressing their gratitude to him for his work on their behalf; and in the outer lights and above the heads of the human figures are angels.

This window is by Messrs. Wilson & Whitehouse of London, and from the interest of its subject attracts much attention.

The next window to the west has four lights, each of which contains two subjects: in the upper tier, Sts. Stephen, Paul, Barnabas, and Philip; in the lower, the stoning of St. Stephen, the Conversion of Saul, St. Paul and Barnabas, and St. Paul before Agrippa. It was given by Stephen Smith in memory of his two sisters, Lucinda and Marie, who died in 1881 and 1883 respectively. This window is the work of Messrs. Burlison & Grylls.

The next window contains, in two tiers, representations of various Old and New Testament characters. It was inserted as a memorial to Samuel and Elizabeth Pickup. It is by Messrs. Clayton & Bell.

The next window also has two subjects in each of its four lights: the upper one, Feeding the hungry, etc.; the lower, the story of the Good Samaritan. This was given in memory of James Pickup, who died in 1868. It is by Messrs. Clayton & Bell.

The next bay opens into the north porch and does not contain any window. Between this and the west wall is a four-light window containing representations of eight incidents in the life of Joseph: 1, His dream; 2, his coat dipped in blood; 3, his imprisonment; 4, his interpretation of the butler's and baker's dreams; 5, his interpretation of Pharaoh's dreams; 6, his honour in Egypt; 7, his turning aside from his brothers to weep; 8, the presentation of Jacob to Pharaoh. This window was presented by J. Beard in 1887, and is by Hardman.

The west window of the outer north aisle has seven lights. The subject is the Ascension. It is a memorial to William Rose, superintendent of the Manchester Fire Brigade, who died in 1884, and is the work of Messrs. Clayton & Bell.

The window at the west end of the inner north aisle has two tiers of subjects; in the heads are angels playing on musical instruments. It was given as a memorial by the widow and children of Samuel Fletcher, who died in 1863, and is by Hardman.

The windows of the clerestory contain five lights; in the north side all are painted, on the south side only the four western ones.

The subjects are:—

On the north side: 1, Aaron sacrificing on the day of Atonement; given by R. B. M. Lingard Monk. It was painted by Messrs. Clayton & Bell.

2. Joshua at the fall of Jericho; given by Sir J.W. Maclure, Bart., M.P. It is by Messrs. Clayton & Bell.

3. David praising God in the tabernacle; given by G. Benton. By Burlison & Grylls.

4. Solomon praising God; given by Susanna Woodcock in memory of Henry Woodcock. By Gibbs of London.

5. The ascent of Elijah; given by Sir W. Cunliffe Brooks, Bart. Painted by Messrs. Clayton & Bell.

6. Malachi pointing out the promised messenger; given by Edward and Henry Charlewood. It was painted by Messrs. Burlison & Grylls.

On the south side:—

1. Moses with the tables of the Law; given by James Chadwick.

2. Miriam dancing and singing; given by William Hatton.

3. Joseph and his brethren; given by Lord Egerton of Tatton.

4. Abraham offering Isaac; given by the Earl of Ellesmere. These four windows are all the work of Messrs. Heaton, Butler & Baynes.

In the choir clerestory on the north side only the second from the west is painted; it represents Christ raising the dead, and is by Clayton & Bell.

On the south side, the first and third from the west are painted. The former represents Christ and Nicodemus; it was the gift of Canon Gibson, and is by Hardman. The other, representing the presentation of Christ in the Temple, was given by Canon Gibson, and is by Ward & Hughes.

The east window of the choir, a short wide window of seven lights, representing the Crucifixion, was given by W. Andrews in 1856, and is by Hardman.

THE NAVE FROM THE WEST.

CHAPTER IV.

SHORT HISTORY OF THE PARISH AND DIOCESE.

Before 1422 the church was purely parochial, and was under rectors, the names of thirteen of whom have come down to us.

Ranulphus de Welling is the first of whom we have any record. Albert de Neville's name is also preserved, but we do not know the dates of their appointment; all we know is that the former lived before the commencement of the thirteenth century. With the appointment of Peter Greslet in 1261, the unbroken list begins.

1284 William de Marchia succeeded him. He became Bishop of Bath and Wells in 1292 or 1293. Here he obtained a great reputation for saintly life, and after his death miracles were worked at his tomb, persons suffering from toothache resorting to it. He was for some time Treasurer of England under Edward I.

1292 Walter de Langton was appointed rector of Manchester, and also Treasurer of England. In 1296 he was promoted to the Bishopric of Lichfield, to which diocese Manchester then belonged. At Lichfield he distinguished himself as builder of the Lady Chapel and Palace. He retained the rectory of Manchester until 1299, when he was succeeded by his grandson.

1301 Geoffrey de Stoke became rector, and was succeeded in 1313 by John de Guerden, whose name appears in several other forms Verdun and Everden. He became Dean of St. Paul's, London, in 1323. Another name, that of John de Arden, occurs about this time among the rectors of Manchester, but the date of his appointment is not known.

1323 Adam de Southwick became rector.

1327 John de Clandon.

1351 Thomas de Wyke; and finally in

1373 Thomas de la Warre.

In 1422 the church became collegiate, when Henry V. granted a charter to Thomas, Lord de la Warre, Rector of Manchester, and Lord of the Manor "Ecclesiam de Mancestre in ecclesiam collegeatam erigere," and from this date the title of Rector was exchanged for that of Warden.

The following is a complete list of the wardens, with the dates of their appointments:—

1422. John Huntington, B.D. (rector of Ashton-under-Lyne); he is noteworthy as the builder of much of the church which we see to-day.

1459. John Booth, LL.B., archdeacon of Redmore, formerly treasurer of the cathedral church at York.

1465. Ralph Langley, LL.D., rector of Prestwich, the rebuilder of the nave.

1481. James Stanley (1), D.D., Prebendary of St Paul's and archdeacon of Chester.

1485. James Stanley (2), M.A., D.C.L. He founded the Chapel of St. John the Baptist, built the entrance to the chapter house, and in connection with Richard Beck, a Manchester merchant, erected the choir stalls and canopies. He became Bishop of Ely in 1509, and is buried in the Ely Chantry at Manchester.

1509. Robert Cliff, B.D., LL.D.

1515. Richard Alday.

1518. George West.

1535. George Collyer, M.A.

1557. Laurence Vaux, B.D., chaplain to the Bishop of Gloucester.

1558. William Bird, M.A.

1570. Thomas Herle, chaplain to Queen Elizabeth.

1578. John Walton, B.D. He was appointed Bishop of Exeter in 1579.

1579. William Chadderton, D.D., consecrated Bishop of Chester in 1579. Manchester by this time had become part of the new see of Chester, and Chadderton retained his wardenship along with the higher office, but he resigned it when he was translated to the see of Lincoln in 1595.

1595. John Dee, M.A., a layman and a celebrated mathematician, alchemist, astrologer, and necromancer, who professed to see visions in crystal globes, and was much consulted by many, among them by the Queen, to forecast future events, held the office of warden for some years, but retired in 1608, and died in poverty at Mortlake, at the age of 81.

1608. Richard Murray, D.D., Rector of Stopford, and Dean of St. Buryan's in Cornwall.

1636. Richard Heyrick, M.A. He was expelled in 1646, but reinstated in his office in 1660. His memorial tablet may be seen on the wall of the south aisle, dated 1667.

1667. Nicholas Stratford, D.D. He resigned in 1684, and five years after this was consecrated Bishop of Chester.

1684. Richard Wroe, D.D., Prebendary of Chester.

1718. Samuel Peploe (1), D.D. He was consecrated Bishop of Chester in 1726, and ruled that see till 1752. He retained the wardenship, together with the bishopric, until 1738.

1738. Samuel Peploe (2), LL.D. He was Chancellor of Chester, and Archdeacon of Richmond, Yorkshire.

1781. Richard Assheton, D.D.

1800. Thomas Blackburne, LL.D.

1823. Thomas Calvert, D.D., rector of Wilmslow.

1840. The Hon. William Herbert, D.D., LL.D. When the diocese of Manchester was formed out of that of Chester in 1847, the warden was raised to the higher rank of Dean, and hence Dr. Herbert was last warden and first Dean, but he did not hold the latter office long.

The following is a list of the Deans:—

1847. The Hon. William Herbert, D.D., LL.D.

1847. George Hull Bowers, D.D.

1872. Benjamin Morgan Cowie, D.D. In 1884 he became Dean of Exeter, a post he held until he died in 1900.

1884. John Oakley, D.D. He had been Dean of Carlisle from 1881-1884.

1890. Edward Craig Maclure, D.D., the present Dean.

The present cathedral staff consists of the Dean, four residentiary Canons, twenty-four honorary Canons, two minor Canons, two Clerks (in orders), an organist, four singing men, and four singing boys on the foundation, to whom others are added by subscription.

The relation of the Dean of Manchester to the Rectory is defined by the Parish of Manchester Division Act, 1850, which states that "Such Part or Residue of the said Parish of Manchester as shall remain after severance therefrom of any Parts or Portions thereof, shall be, and be deemed to be for all Ecclesiastical Purposes, the Parish of Manchester; and the Dean of Manchester for the time being shall, upon Institution and Installation into his Deanery, have the cure of souls therein, and shall be assisted in such cure by the Chaplains or Minor Canons of the said Cathedral or Collegiate Church, to be hereafter appointed, who, in all matters connected with the Spiritual Duties of the said Parish, shall be subject to, and act under his directions; and the said Dean shall have all rights and powers in reference to the performance of the services of the said church, as the Parish Church of Manchester, as fully and effectually as if he were Rector of the same, subject nevertheless to any rights belonging to or duties imposed on the Canons and Minor Canons or Chaplains of the said Cathedral or Collegiate Church, in respect of the performance of the services thereof prescribed by the recited Letters Patent."

The list of the churchwardens of the parish church from 1422 to 1595, and from 1663 to the present time, three for each year, is in existence.

The diocese of Manchester has but a short history, as it has had an independent existence for little more than half a century.

Until 1541 Manchester was part of the great see of Lichfield. In that year Henry VIII. made a new diocese of Chester, by taking the archdeaconry of Chester from the diocese of Lichfield, and the archdeaconry of Richmond from that of York.

The see of Chester then included the counties of Chester, Lancaster, and portions of Cumberland, Westmorland, York, Flint, and Denbigh.

In 1836 the archdeaconry of Richmond was assigned to the new see of Ripon, and the part of Lancashire known as Furness, together with these parts of Westmorland and Cumberland above mentioned, were added to the diocese of Carlisle.

In 1847 the new see of Manchester was formed from the diocese of Chester.

The diocese of Manchester lies within the county of Lancaster, but does not embrace the whole county, part of which forms the see of Liverpool, while a small part of it belongs to that of Carlisle.

It consists of three archdeaconries:—Manchester, Lancaster, and Blackburn.

The total number of benefices in the diocese in the year 1900 was 550, of beneficed clergy, 525, and of assistant curates about 360.

The cathedral church is calculated to afford accommodation for 2000 persons.

Since the foundation of the see it has been presided over by three bishops.

The first was the Right Rev. **James Prince Lee**, D.D., F.R.S., for many years headmaster of King Edward's School, Birmingham, and a distinguished scholar. He was elected in 1847, and consecrated in the first month of the following year by the Archbishop of York and the Bishops of Chester and Worcester. He died in 1869 at Mauldeth Hall, Heaton Mersey, and was buried in Heaton Mersey Churchyard.

He was succeeded by the Right Rev. **James Fraser**, D.D., who when at Oxford had gained the Ireland Scholarship, and became a Fellow of Oriel College. He was a man of great intellectual power, of kindly manner, and won the respect and confidence not only of Churchmen, but of members of all denominations, especially of the mill hands of his populous diocese. He was nominated to the see in January 1890, and consecrated in March of the same year. He died 22nd October 1885 at Manchester, and is buried in the churchyard of Ufton Nervet, Berks.

The present bishop, the Right Rev. **James Moorhouse**, D.D., was translated from the see of Melbourne to that of Manchester in 1886.

DIMENSIONS OF MANCHESTER CATHEDRAL.

	Ft.
Total length over all, exterior,	248
Width,	173
Length of Nave and Choir, interior,	172
Width of Nave exclusive of Projections, interior,	114
Distance from Rood Screen to Screen of Lady Chapel,	88

Length and breadth of Tower, exterior exclusive of buttresses,	28
Length of Lady Chapel, E. to W., interior,	18
Width of Lady Chapel, N. to S., interior,	19
Width of Nave,	27
Width of inner Nave Aisles,	16
Width of outer North Aisle of Nave,	24
Width of outer South Aisle of Nave,	22
Projection South Porch beyond Wall of aisle, exclusive of buttresses,	22
Projecting of North Porch, beyond walls of aisle, exclusive of buttresses,	25
Width of South Porch, interior,	11
Width of North Porch, interior,	13
Diameter of Chapter House interior,	19
Height of Roof, interior,	50
Height of Tower,	140

Area, about 18,000 sq. ft.

CHETHAM'S HOSPITAL AND LIBRARY

THE HALL, CHETHAM'S HOSPITAL.

CHETHAM'S HOSPITAL FROM THE SOUTH-EAST.

CHETHAM'S HOSPITAL AND LIBRARY.

As we stand on the north side of the cathedral and look to the north, our eyes rest upon a wide gravelled courtyard beyond a low wall, backed up by a range of mediaeval-looking buildings. These were the domestic buildings of the College, and are now used partly for Chetham's Free Library, partly for the school known as Chetham's Hospital. The endowment and other sources of income provide for the board and education of a hundred boys. They receive a sound elementary education, and are instructed in technical and manual work. The school is carried on under the Board of Education, and is typical of this education at its best. The religious instruction is in accordance with the tenets of the Established Church, and much care is taken to train the boys not only in intellectual and manual pursuits, but in morals and manners. A boy once placed on the foundation of Humphrey Chetham has a successful career assured to him, unless he forfeits his chances by subsequent folly on his own part. The boys who show the greatest intellectual power can be passed on to the Manchester Grammar School, and thence to Owens College, while the feoffees of the hospital have no difficulty in finding good places in the business houses of Manchester for the rest. To have been educated at Chetham's Hospital is a great recommendation to any boy. The boys still wear the picturesque costume of the sixteenth century—caps, bands, long-skirted dark blue coats, knee-breeches, stockings, and shoes adorned with buckles. The visitor to the Hospital will probably be greeted by one of these boys, who will ask if he wishes to see the buildings. The boy will, if the answer is in the affirmative, take the visitor to the library, where, on payment of sixpence, a ticket will be handed to him, franking him for the day, and the boy will conduct him over the whole of the buildings, pointing out the past and present uses to which each part of them was or is put.

Before we proceed to describe the building a few words must be said about its history.

Its site was once occupied by the "summer camp" of Roman legionaries, and when the Romans passed away from the island, it is highly probable that the English occupants of the country used it as a place of abode. The first authentic notice of its occupation by any person whose name has come down to us, dates from 1182, when Robert, the fifth Baron Greslet, kept court here. Thomas, the eighth baron, granted the citizens of Manchester their first charter in 1301, signing and sealing the charter here. He was the last male in the direct line of descent, and on his death the property passed to John De la Warre, who was a descendant of the Greslets or Gresleys in the female line. One of his descendants, Thomas, as has been already mentioned, became rector of Manchester, who before his death applied to King Henry V. for a charter to enable him to collegiate the church. He bestowed on it lands to increase the endowment, and gave his baronial hall to the newly founded college of priests to be used as their residence. All this may be read in the grant made in the first year of Henry VI. Certain alterations were made in the buildings, to fit them for the new use to which they were to be put, and from 1422 to 1549 they were occupied by warden after warden, who, assisted by the Fellows, performed the services in the adjoining church, looked after the sick and poor, and ministered generally to the inhabitants of the parish of Manchester. For some reason the College was not suppressed in the reign of Henry VIII., when the revenues of monasteries, small and great, were seized by the king; but in the first year of Edward VI. it was disendowed, and in the third year of the reign it was granted to Edward Stanley, third Earl of Derby. He used it as a town house. Henry Stanley, the next earl, in the reign of Elizabeth obtained a charter from the Queen, re-endowing the College, and it once more became the abode of the wardens, now priests of the reformed Church. During the civil wars the warden was expelled (1646), and the buildings seized by the Parliament. They were let to a certain Joseph Werden, who sublet the refectory to the Presbyterians, to be used by them as a meeting-house. The Independents made use of a barn in the enclosure for a similar purpose.

THE NORTH GALLERY OF THE CLOISTER.

Lieut.-Col. the Rev. John Wigan applied for the reversion of this property, "part of y^e estate of the late Earl of Derby, and part of y^e jointure of y^e Countess Dowager already sequestrated."

Humphrey Chetham also had his eye upon this property, wishing to obtain it so that he might carry out a project formed long before to found a school and home for boys. The survey of the property made at this time describes it as consisting of "Y^e large building called ye College in Manchester, consisting of many rooms, with two barnes, one gate house, verie much decay'd, one parcell of ground formerly an orchard, and one garden, now in ye possession of Joseph Werden gent., who pays for ye same, for ye use of the Common wealth, ten pounds yearly. There is likewise one other room in ye said College reserved and made use of for publique meetings of X'sian conscientious people."

Humphrey Chetham did not live to see the school founded; but in his will, made three years before his death, which took place in 1653, he appointed trustees to carry out his purpose. They, in accordance with his instructions, bought "ye great house with buildings, court, gardens, and appurtenances, called ye Colledge or the Colledge House," obtaining it for the sum of £500.

On August 5, 1658, the building was formally dedicated to its new use, and Hallworth, chief assistant to Heyrick, the expelled warden, who, as stated in Chapter IV., was afterwards reinstated, in his speech on this occasion, told the history of the building, and concluded by saying, "Henceforth the said house could fitly and justly be named by no other name than by the name of Mr. Chetham's Hospital," and by that name it is known at the present day.

At the time of the Restoration the Stanleys claimed the property of which they had been dispossessed by the Parliament, but made no difficulty about regranting to the feoffees that part of it occupied by the new School and Library. For the Library as well as the School had been already founded, since after making sufficient provision for the maintenance of the Hospital, the feoffees had money in hand which they spent in the purchase of books, thus forming the nucleus of the first *free* library in England. To this collection books have been added by gift, bequest, and purchase, so that the library now contains about 60,000 volumes. The books can be consulted free of charge during certain hours of the day, but are not allowed to be removed from the building. The general public, however, does not make much use of the library, as it does not contain the light and ephemeral literature that appeals to modern taste; but the student who desires to read up some special subject will find many valuable books and manuscripts to aid him in his work. Among the rare books is a copy of the historical compilations of Matthew Paris, with marginal corrections in the author's handwriting.

There is much matter to be found on these shelves dealing with the antiquities and history of Lancashire and Cheshire. Canon Raine bequeathed a fine series of Lancashire manuscripts; besides these may be seen a collection of broadsides, formed by Mr. T. O. Halliwell-Phillipps, and the library of John Byrom. In the last named collection is the final draft of the well-known hymn, "Christians, awake; salute the happy morn." Among the other books there are some fine specimens of Caxton's printing.

THE COLLEGE GATEWAY.

We leave the churchyard, cross the street that skirts it to the north, and pass through a small doorway in the wall at the opposite side of the street, and so enter the play-ground of Chetham's Hospital. On our left hand as we make our way to the original building, we pass the modern schoolroom, which stands by itself. This, like many other buildings in Manchester, was designed by A. Waterhouse, R.A. The main building runs east and west, with projecting wings at either end. Near the eastern wing we notice the old entrance gateway, and the modern staircase leading up to what was the "hospitium" or guest-house. This has been converted into a dormitory for the boys. The most interesting part of the College is to be found in the western wing, of which an illustration is given, p. 63. The three windows crossed by transoms are those of the hall; the lower windows to the left of these belong to the audit room, the upper to the warden's private room, now the reading-room of the library. The building to the extreme left contains the library on the upper floor, and offices on the lower.

CORRIDOR AND ENTRANCE TO THE HALL.

There is a long corridor, shown in the illustration below, running from east and west of the building; it can be entered by a door at its eastern end not shown in the illustration on p. 63. After entering this, as we proceed towards the west we pass on the right hand the fine kitchen; it has an open timbered roof about 35 feet from floor to ridge, and measures 29 feet in length and 17 in width; beyond this, on the same side, are two doors giving entrance to the cellar, where the warden and Fellows kept their wine, the buttery or rather *butlery*. Opposite this, on the left hand side, is the Hall; its north end is partially closed by massive screens of black oak. It has windows on the east and west. One of those on the west gives light to a staircase with Jacobean balusters, which, starting in a direction parallel to the west wall of the hall, turns round and gives access to the upper story. As we still pass westward we come to the cloister on the left hand, and the old infirmary on the right; and a door still further on leads out into a garden, where the fish pond was formerly situated; in this the fish required for Fridays and other days of abstinence were kept. Caught in other water—the streams of Irwell and Irk probably—they were brought here and stored so that they could always be caught without difficulty when required for the table.

THE CLOISTER—SOUTH-WEST ANGLE.

The cloister is small and has only three walks, the one to the north forming part of the corridor which has been just described; the one to the west is terminated at its south end by an iron gate; and the walk on the south leads to, and is terminated by the entrance to the audit room. From the west walk (illustration, p. 83) an archway leads into the cloister itself. This is a very secluded spot, and the walls show signs of great age. This cloister has one peculiarity: the walks already described have other walks or corridors over them. Over the south walk is a corridor leading by what was St. Mary's Chapel into the warden's room; the corridor over the west walk opened out into what was once the dormitory, now filled with bookcases; the walk over the long eastern corridor below gave access to the old refectory, which has now been divided into living-rooms for the governor and the librarian.

The long straight line of building between the eastern and western wing contained the old school, the brew house, and the bakery; the upper story, used formerly for guests, has been converted into a dormitory for the boys; this is the most ancient part of the hospital.

The reader, from the sketch just given, will understand the general arrangement of the building, various parts of which will now be described in more detail.

We will begin with the **Hall**. This measures 43 feet from north to south, 24 from east to west; its walls are 22 feet in height, and the distance from the floor to the ridge of the open timber roof is 35 feet.

At the south end is the dais, behind this the wall is panelled; on the west side near the dais is a recess shown in the illustration on page 72, and on the same side of the hall, further north, and in the centre of the wall, is the "Ingle-nook," as it is called.

RECESS IN THE HALL.

This Ingle-nook did not originally form part of the hall. It is said that at one time it was a barn, or place for storing grain for use in the baronial buildings.

The hall was in all probability warmed, according to the usual custom, by a brazier standing on the centre of the floor, the smoke from which gathered under the high pitched roof, blackening beams and rafters, and finally escaped through a spire or turret rising from the ridge of the roof furnished with louvre boards. The fireplace was at some subsequent time removed to the west side of the room, and afterwards placed inside the ingle-nook, first at the back of it, then at the north-eastern corner.

It will be seen from the illustration that this recess was at one time entered through an arch, but the sides of this were afterwards cut away and a flat lintel, composed of two enormous stones, was inserted; the space between this and the arch was then filled in with masonry; at the same time, no doubt, the interior space was covered with a plaster ceiling at a height of about six feet from the floor; this has been recently removed, and the roof vaulted with stone. The recess is lighted from the back with windows, and provided with seats, and has an open fireplace. The ingle-nook is a picturesque addition to the hall, and forms no doubt a very cosy corner when on a cold day the fire is blazing in the grate; but as a means of warming the hall the present arrangement is manifestly far inferior to the old plan of having an open fire in the centre of the floor of the hall.

On the wall above this recess may be seen a bust of the founder, with crossed swords on either side of it, and a flintlock hung below it. The illustrations show that the walls are built of large-size squared stones, and are not covered with plaster. Across the end of the hall, cutting off the western part of it to form the main passage spoken of above, is a battlemented screen. This is peculiar in that it is not a continuous screen furnished with doorways for entrance, and does not rise to the level of the roof, but consists of three detached pieces, one resting against the east, one against the west wall, and one standing in the middle, each rising to the height of about nine feet. Thus two entrances, each about five feet wide, are left. Here, as in other parts of the building, the improvements of the nineteenth century have found their way, and the mediaeval walls of the old hall are lighted with electric lamps—a most convenient and safe addition, but striking one, at first, as out of harmony with the surroundings. Sundry portraits adorn the walls, the floor is neatly sanded, and the room is kept scrupulously clean; an air of refinement is added to it by vases of fresh flowers placed on the table. In this hall the boys of the Hospital assemble at stated hours for prayers and meals.

WEST SIDE OF THE CLOISTER.

The next part to be examined is the cloister court. This is a very small enclosure, surrounded by somewhat high walls. Admission to it is obtained from the west walk through the archway cut in one of the windows, shown in the illustration. The curious form of the glass in the windows is worthy of note; the pavement of the cloister-garth is formed of cobblestones, and towards the south end may be seen the top of the college well. The cloister is not rectangular, the line of the eastern side being broken by sundry projections.

STAIRCASE LEADING TO CLOISTER GALLERY.

As we leave the cloister, we examine the walks to the south and west. The latter (see illustration, p. 83) is terminated at its south end by a wrought iron gate through which we get a glimpse of the outside view and the entrance to the library. The roof is nearly flat, with massive oaken beams. Several doors may be seen on the western side opening into cells—the living-rooms of the clergy connected with the college. As we turn round the corner and pass into the south walk, we see before us the door of the audit room. The oaken ceiling of this room is of fifteenth century date; the walls up to a certain height are wainscoted; above this they are covered with a plaster frieze. Here may be seen what is known as the "Founder's Chair," although it is of far earlier date than Chetham's time—earlier, indeed, than the date of the conversion of the baron's residence into a college in the fifteenth century.

CLOISTER GALLERY, NORTH SIDE.

Leaving this room, we pass through the two cloister walks already described, and proceed towards the hall until on the right hand we see a staircase with balusters of oak, black from age. We mount this, and when we reach the top find ourselves in the upper corridor that runs along the north side of the cloister-garth. This is lit by windows looking into the cloister, and is covered with a wooden ceiling, just at the head of the staircase is the doorway leading into the private rooms of the governor, with exquisite oak fittings; on the north side of this corridor are doors similar to those that we noticed in the corridor below, opposite to the hall; these lead into the librarian's rooms; beyond these, to the west, stands a beautiful Tudor table of carved oak. At the west end of the corridor is an iron studded door. The carvings over the doorway on the west side should not be passed by unnoticed (see p. 65). The corridor over the west walk of the cloister is filled with bookcases plentifully supplied with books.

CHETHAM'S LIBRARY, FORMERLY THE DORMITORY.

Parallel to this runs the old dormitory of the College, a room with a fine timber roof lighted from above; on the west side of this are a number of compartments formed of tall bookcases, and entered from the corridor by open-work doors. At the north end of the corridor is a window filled with painted glass, one light of which represents St. Martin of Tours dividing his cloak with a beggar, and the other Eutychus falling out of the window.

At the south end of this corridor we find a staircase which leads from the ground floor close to the main entrance to the library, and is, in fact, the way by which readers usually enter it. There is a room with a similar timber roof running along the south side of the building parallel to the corridor above the south walk of the cloister. This was once a chapel dedicated to St. Mary, and now, like the dormitory, is filled with bookcases; but an oak altar rail, dating from the middle of the sixteenth century, with double spiral rails, may still be seen here.

At the east end of the south corridor is a door leading into a beautiful room, now used as the reading room; formerly it was the warden's room, and many a man well known in history has sat within its walls. Here Sir Walter Raleigh and the courtiers of his day were entertained by the warden, Dr. Dee, of whom mention was made in the last chapter,—a wizard as he was then thought to be, whom even the Queen did not hesitate to consult when she wished to know the future.

This room, like many others in this building, has an open timber roof and a cornice, dating from the time of the foundation of the College in the days of Henry V. The walls are wainscoted up to the level of the spring of the roof which spans the room from east to west.

THE WARDEN'S ROOM, NOW THE READING ROOM—NORTH SIDE.

In the centre of the north side of this room is a fireplace. This wall is wainscoted up to the same height as the other walls, and above the oak panelling it is profusely decorated, as will be seen from the illustrations, with scrolls and other patterns. This decoration was done in the early years of the reign of Charles II., after the College had been converted into Chetham's Hospital. In the centre of the room is a handsome oval oak table, with a number of chairs to match; against the south wall stands a fifteenth century communion table, and against the north wall to the left of the fireplace, a handsome sideboard of carved oak. This was made up of portions of two pieces of old furniture, namely, the top of a bookcase once given by Humphrey Chetham to Walmsley Church, near Bolton-le-Moors, still bearing an inscription: "The gift of Humphrey Chetham Esquire, 1655," and a fifteenth century bedstead once used by the Pretender when sleeping at Hulton Park in Lancashire. This sideboard was presented to the College by a member of the Hulton family, who was one of the Chetham feoffees. Round the walls are several portraits. From the east side of the room there is a projecting bay lighted by three windows and furnished with seats and a square writing table with sloping sides, to which students can take the book from which they wish to make extracts. The enrichments of the ceiling of the bay are of plaster, but the rest of the vault is stone. All the floors of this upper story are of oak, well polished by the feet of many generations. The furniture of the reading room harmonizes well with the room itself. The windows are placed under widely splayed, obtusely pointed four centred arches. On the sill of one stands a statuette in bronze of Humphrey Chetham and one of the boys of his school, similar to the marble statue already described as standing at the east end of the north choir aisle of the cathedral church. At the northwest corner of the room is a door which the visitor might easily overlook, but which gives access to a most interesting chamber. This was at one time the minstrels' gallery opening out into the hall, when in the time of the Greslets and the De le Warres, the baron, his guests and retainers feasted merrily there, while the harpers twanged their strings and sang of deeds of daring and war and victory. When the building passed into ecclesiastical hands in 1422 the arches opening into the hall were walled up, and the minstrels' gallery was converted into a scriptorium; two small openings were, however, left in the wall from which the warden passing out of his own room into the scriptorium might see what was being done in the hall below.

THE READING ROOM: EAST SIDE.

Leaving the warden's room we may descend by the staircase at the southwest corner of the building, and before quitting this part of the hospital altogether, make a closer examination of the wrought iron gate at the south end of the west walk of the cloister. On it we see embossed in brass, the arms of the founder and below the arms, the motto, "Quod tuum tene," "Hold thine own."

The part of the building used as the boys' dormitories has been internally refitted in modern times, and so has lost somewhat of its archaeological interest; but the building, taken as a whole, is a very valuable relic of mediaeval times. Even if there were nothing older than Chetham's day, it would be well worth study; but of course it is of much earlier date, and we see a building which has been used for three distinct purposes at different times of its history: first as a baron's dwelling-place, then as the abode of one of those religious bodies differing in many points from the regular monastic orders known as colleges of clergy, and finally converted into one of those educational establishments which sprang up into vigorous existence in the days succeeding the dissolution of the monasteries. It is especially interesting to note how many features of the life led by the boys at the time of the foundation are still preserved at this hospital. Modern improvements have been judiciously introduced into the management of this educational foundation; there has been no unnecessary reckless sweeping away of what is old and picturesque, and yet, at the same time, the character of the education given has been brought well up to modern requirements, fulfilling literally the conditions laid down by the founder, who directed that "Ye boys shall be taught ye reading, ye writing, ye summes, and all kinds of ye ingenuitie."

THE CLOISTER—WEST WALK.

It is a matter of congratulation that this ancient building has been preserved from falling into ruin and being used as a quarry of ready-hewn stone, a fate that overtook so many of the religious houses of the country when the monastic bodies were expelled; and also that by the wise regulations made for the admission of visitors, the place is easily seen, and yet is preserved from all chance of injury.

GROUND-PLAN OF THE COLLEGIATE BUILDINGS, NOW CHETHAM'S HOSPITAL.

(From "Old Halls of Lancashire and Cheshire," by Henry Taylor.)

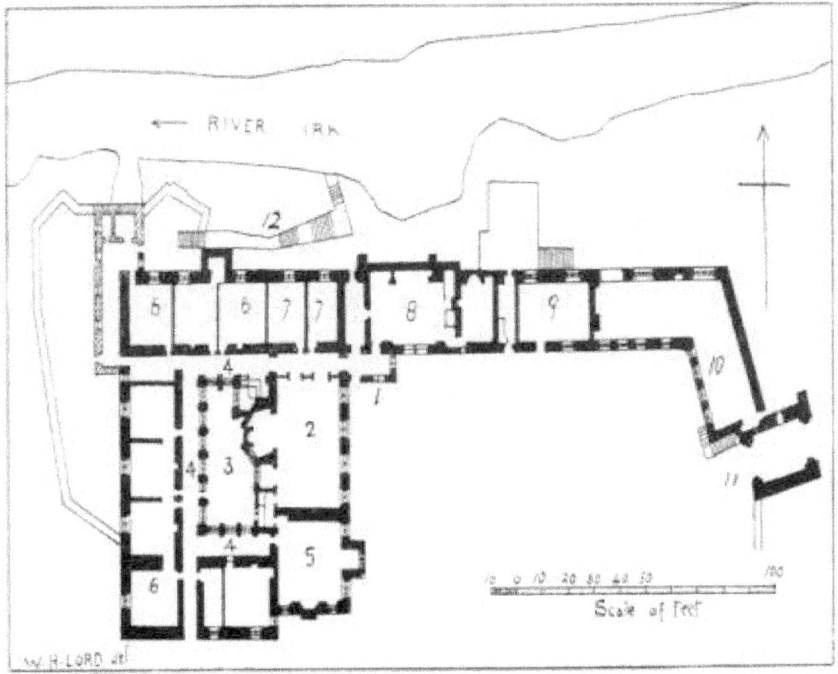

1. Porch. 2. Hall. 3. Cloister. 4. Cloister walks with galleries above. 5. Audit Room with Warden's Room above. 6. Fellows' Rooms. 7. Butteries. 8. Kitchen. 9. Bakehouse. 10. Hospitium. 11. Gateway. 12. Steps to River—now covered.

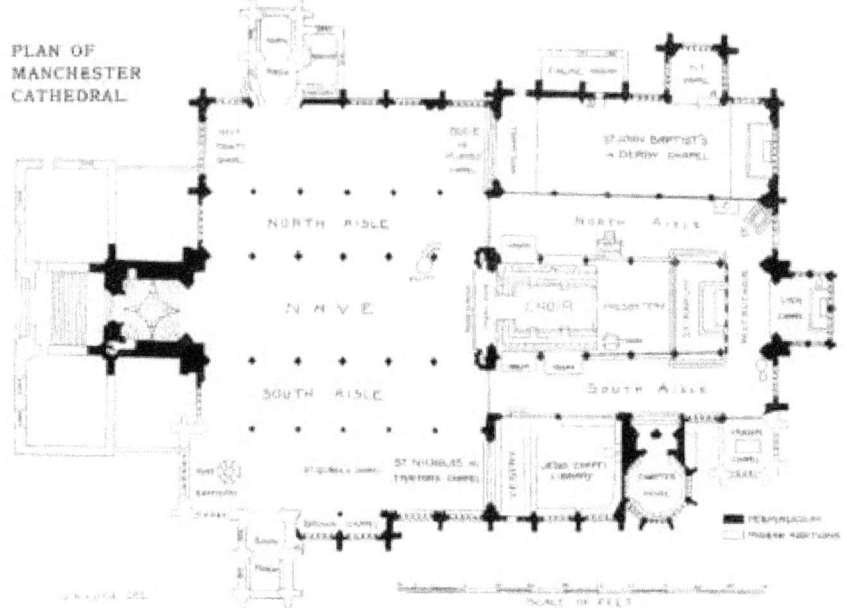

PLAN OF MANCHESTER CATHEDRAL.

FOOTNOTES

1 It states that the churches of St. Mary and St. Michael hold one carucate (that is, about 100 acres) of land quit of all taxes save the Danegelt.

2 A triforium in purely Perpendicular buildings is rare.

3 The height of the central line of the roof (50 feet) is not quite double the span (27 feet).

4 St. George and St. Denys, patron saints of England and France, were added to the dedication at the time that the church became collegiate, Henry V. being King of England and France.

Milton Keynes UK
Ingram Content Group UK Ltd.
UKHW010311220224
438247UK00004B/453